My Headless Marriage

IF I KNEW THEN WHAT I KNOW NOW

Zelda D. Oliver-Miles

FIVE CHOSEN OAKS PUBLISHING
Adamsville, AL

Copyright © 2021 by Zelda D. Oliver-Miles.

All rights reserved. No part of this publication may be reproduced, distributed or transmitted in any form or by any means, including photocopying, recording, or other electronic or mechanical methods, without the prior written permission of the publisher, except in the case of brief quotations embodied in critical reviews and certain other noncommercial uses permitted by copyright law.

Five Chosen Oaks Publishing

Unless otherwise indicated, all Scripture quotations are from the King James Version, public domain.

My Headless Marriage. -- 1st ed.
ISBN 978-0-578-84774-0

Contents

Don't Take It Lightly 7

To Have and to Hold 15

Leave 23

Cleave 33

Becoming One 45

Headship 55

A Final Word 66

DISCUSSION QUESTIONS 68

Scripture Index 70

About the Author 72

This is dedicated to the One who inspired and instructed that it be written. I pray that it honors and glorifies Jesus Christ and heals readers' broken places.

ACKNOWLEDGMENTS

My heart is full as I say thank you to all the people who helped me throughout the writing process – from listening to the idea to pushing me to finish it.

To Wendell, my husband of 31 years, thank you for space and patience as I got this done. It was hard, but nothing worth fighting for ever is. To my loving son, Yori, and my cheerleader daughter, Xenia - Momma loves you so much. Forgive me for not always being a good example.

To my parents, Annie and Arthur Brown, thank you for foundational beginnings. I still have a lot to learn.

Arthurene, Andre and Arthur, if only you understood how much I want to see you guys win.

Dr. Dadron Deon, my pusher and mentor. I don't evenknow where to begin.

Kisha Black and Inesse Semeah– Every time I heard from you my heart swelled (and I cried just a little). Thank you for being so encouraging.

Valerie Johnson Brown, Esq. – My sister you rock with a red pen!

Shout out to Breaire Strayhorne of Pauline's Fine Cakes and Desserts for the bomb cake on the cover.

"May your love be modern enough to survive the times and old-fashioned enough to last forever."

—UNKNOWN

INTRODUCTION

Unlike most young women, I had no fairy tale dreams or ideas about a big wedding day nor was I expecting Prince Charming. I'd said many times that I'd never get married. I never thought marriage was in my future. Everything I saw and heard about marriage did not appeal to me. All the people I was exposed to either argued all the time, didn't look happy or were saying without saying it — their faces said it all because their husbands were cheating, smacking them around or weren't at all loving towards them. Love and affection were rarely shown. Why would anyone want to subject themselves to that life? But as time changes so do thoughts and feelings. I can't say with certainty when my thoughts about marriage and family changed, but they did.

My husband always tells people that the day he met me he knew I was his wife. That baffles me because on the day we met, I called him "an arrogant son of a bitch." Yes, I had a potty mouth. Besides that, he was interrupting my dinner, the first home-cooked meal I'd had since leaving home for college. It hadn't mattered that he had sexy, long eyelashes and beautiful brown eyes. I was only interested in the plate of shrimp, hush puppies, and fries sitting in front of me. I kept thinking, "why is he talking to me when he seems to know at least one of the other young ladies at the table. Why doesn't he go back and sit with his roommate; that's who he came here with . . . ugh."

It would be a month or so later before we'd meet again. When we did we spent hours sharing our life stories. In one night, I felt I knew everything there was to know about him. His openness was intoxicating. Not only that he seemed to be listening to me. When he walked me back to my dorm, he said he would call me. I remember getting to my room and dropping on the bed feeling happy, then sad. My roommate notices and asks what was wrong. "He said he'd call but he didn't ask for my phone number." I remember whispering a prayer, "Lord, if this is meant to happen let him find a way to call me." I was like a child at the Willy Wonka Chocolate Factory the next day when he called." How was I to know that giddy girl would marry that man, have children with him and over the years contemplate "why did I get married?"

I can't tell you how many times I've asked myself this question during our 30 years of marriage. However, I admit that when I've asked this question, it has been out of a place of hurt, disappointment, fear, and/or selfishness. And it is not because I don't love him. It was in deep moments of despair that I received some painful revelations. They were not about why I married the man nor what was wrong with him. But the revelations were unequivocally about what was wrong with me and why I had issues with some aspects of marriage and not others.

Not until recently have I come to better understand God's principles of marriage because for years I guess you can say I was rebelling against "headship" and "submission" as I knew them. In action, these two terms looked and sounded more like control and manipulation, not love or mutual respect. So, I confess, my past behaviors have not resembled what I have been commanded to do as a wife. At times I have been uncooperative, disrespectful, unkind, willful, etcetera because I lacked understanding. It was in the midst of God correcting me that I heard the title for this book, *My Headless Marriage*.

But why headless? The answer wasn't complicated. My husband was "head" in title only and had not been the leader I needed or desired in our marriage. He'd often told me that one of the reasons he married me was because he knew I could take care of myself and would handle all the things he didn't want to. In essence, he'd relinquished much of his responsibilities as husband and I had enabled him by leading when I should have been walking beside him.

I was inspired to look at what we call the "wedding vows" and see how they fit with the three principles of God's plan for marriage. In case you didn't know, there are no wedding vows in the Bible. It is believed that wedding vows originated in England nearly 500 years ago. Archbishop Thomas Cranmer, the architect of the Reformed Church of England, wrote them in a book he called *Book of Common Prayer*. The book is a liturgy for the English Church and is filled with prayers, litanies, holy communion and services, such as baptism, confirmations, marriage and funerals. It is still used today by most religious organizations and during civil ceremonies.

The first wedding included no exchange of vows, but Moses writes in Genesis three principles designed to build and sustain a marriage as well as set the foundation for the family it produces. These principles sound simplistic, but not knowing them or having an understanding of them is what I believe is causing marriages to fail and families to be broken. God's three principles for marriage are these: leave, cleave and become one.

"Therefore shall a man leave his father and his mother, and shall cleave unto his wife: and they shall be one flesh." — Genesis 2:24

I am grateful that God loves me enough to show me where I was going wrong in my marriage. (It took my stubborn self twenty-nine years to ask and listen for an answer.) The revelations and quiet rebukes are what I hope to share and impart, especially to those with trepidations or misguided ideals of what marriage is supposed to look like, as we continue this adventure called marriage. Growing together in marriage through the disagreements, losses and disappointments is the most rewarding work we may ever do in fulfilling God's command of being fruitful and multiplying. My prayer for you is the same as this toast I heard on a Lifetime Christmas movie:

May your marriage be long, your arguments short and your love everlasting. (—2020 Merry Liddle Christmas Wedding)

CHAPTER 1

Don't Take It Lightly

"How many times are you gonna keep giving me your ring back?" he asked after about the third time. This time I'd thrown it at him in frustration over seemingly nothing.

The first time I'd given it back I placed it on the dresser and walked out of his apartment shaking my head repeating, "I can't."

Throughout our two-year engagement, I broke up with and gave back my ring countless times. Now that I look back on those days I realize I was stalling, and afraid. Afraid of finding out after the wedding that my husband wasn't who I thought he was. I was afraid I'd be miserable. Afraid I would be an awful wife and one day, mother. Afraid I'd never live out my dreams even though I had no clear picture of what they were at the time — I was barely twenty-years-old and hadn't yet figured out who I was and I was about to make a decision that was supposed to be for a lifetime. Nevertheless, this uncertainty had me unexcited about doing what most young girls dream of— setting a date and planning a wedding. It was not my dream or plan. The more I put off setting a date, the more anxious it seemed my fiancé got.

"Just tell me when and where to show up," he said each time he brought up the subject.

This was a decision "not to be entered lightly." I understood that, and he said he did, too. Marriage is more than "just a commitment." Marriage is sacred. It is ordained by God. It is a covenant between God, a man and the woman chosen to be his wife. Marriage is not about all the planning, the dress or the day you say I do. Marriage is everything that happens after the vows are made before God and man. Scripture even says marriage "*is a great mystery concerning Christ and the church,"* (Ephesians 5:31-32). A mystery, I believe, because there are many fine details that require a relationship with God so that instructions are heard and applied to each and every situation. One of the many lessons I've learned over the years is that while every marriage is sacred not everything works for/in every marriage and that is by design. We are not clones of each other, in fact, even identical twins differ.

For instance, in one marriage the wife may not work outside the home, but instead manages the home, cares for the children, and receives an allowance from her husband that she is to use on herself. In another marriage the wife works outside the home, shares in paying the bills, and does a majority of the care for the children while the husband though present is not an active participant. Then in another marriage, you may find the wife may or may not work outside the home, but the husband cooks, cleans, and dotes on his wife. He knows her and meets her needs before she asks. What it boils down to is how the husband loves his wife, and how the wife respects and loves him. I didn't know that. It was naive to think that saying I love you equates to knowing how to love.

But I knew very little and was afraid to ask or talk about it with anyone, especially my fiancé. Based on our conversations, I figured he would have fewer answers than I had since both of us had front row seats to some pretty dysfunctional marriages. The difference between us was he embraced the idea of marriage like he did his beloved navy pea coat he bought himself upon entering the United States Air Force Academy after high school. He wore that coat with such pride despite having parted ways with his dream of becoming a pilot.

Talking about getting married made me anxious. Other people's opinions and offers of assistance did not help either. My beloved grandmother was excited about this wedding and went into full planning mode. It didn't matter that I didn't have a date. She was suggesting I ask childhood classmates and church friends to be my bridesmaids. We talked about a menu reminiscent of Sunday dinners — chicken or ham, potato and pasta salad, macaroni and cheese, rolls, pound cake — and wedding colors. I don't remember what my initial color was, but grandmother suggested peach and cream. I started having borderline migraines and mild anxiety episodes. Whenever the topic of the wedding came up, I'd say "let me get through the semester and I'll start planning." One semester turned into another. I kept avoiding the subject and my fiancé's question of whether I'd picked a date. After a while he seemed to accept that I wasn't going to set a date until after graduation. Then a series of events forced my hand.

In the fall of 1989, soldiers were being prepped and put on active duty for a potential war in the Persian

Gulf (Iraq had invaded Kuwait). One of my neighbors, who was set to graduate, informed us that he'd been called up for active duty. Unbeknownst to me, my fiancé worried that his National Guard unit was on the list of units whose services may be needed during this entanglement. He began to press me more about a wedding date and started expressing his concern about my commitment to him. The more he pushed, the more annoyed I got. That annoyance finally turned in to me waving a white flag.

"Have you put any more thought into a date yet?" he asked one weekend still dressed in his Army National Guard uniform.

I rolled my eyes and stared at him. "Next week. Let's just go to the courthouse."

He smiled. "You serious?"

"Yeah," *I returned to my studies.*

My wedding day is a blur. Something made me upset that day. I don't remember what. If it wasn't for the couple of pictures that we have (and my best guess is that my brother-in-law took them) I couldn't tell you that I wore a mustard double-breasted blazer dress, no veil, no hat, or bouquet. When we arrived at the county courthouse, I was still upset. There was no one there to calm me or reassure me — other than my fiancé — that things were going to be okay. So, since the question crossed your mind, I'll answer it. Yes, we eloped. I don't remember what the Justice of Peace said. I do recall that in the few minutes he spoke, my thoughts went from 'I really want to marry him' to 'I don't know about this, so maybe I shouldn't do it.'

But there I stood silent. My way out would have been to raise my hand when the question was asked if anyone knew of a reason the two of us shouldn't be married. But I didn't raise my hand or speak up. This I remember about my wedding day: when we got to the vow exchange and I was asked if I will, there was a long pause before I said I do. It was a struggle to get those two words out, but I did. I remember looking at my fiancé and hearing him release a long, very audible sigh. I guess my pause was too long for him. But he'd chosen me, and I'd accepted. We loved each other. The real question was "now what?"

At twenty-one I was about to be this man's wife. I did not have a clue what that really meant other than cooking, washing and ironing and keeping house for someone that probably would never really appreciate it. I just knew that wasn't going to be my husband because the first time I attempted to iron one of his uniforms, he politely told me he would do it himself.

I had no idea what would come next.

OLIVER-MILES

CHAPTER 2

To Have and to Hold

After the ceremony, I reflected on all the unsolicited advice I'd received after announcing my engagement. Some of it good, but most of it, well ... let's just say it wasn't about "having and holding." I received no instruction on how to respect my husband when I felt disrespected, overlooked, ignored or unappreciated. I received no instruction on how to deal with feeling alone or like I was making all the sacrifices and doing all the work just so "he could show up" when he wanted.

To have and to hold, I've discovered, is all about the promise of unconditional acceptance and physical affection and tenderness; a promise to cherish, value and protect each other. It is one of the principles of God's plan for marriage. It is not a statement of ownership or control for that matter despite what some tend to think because of two words — headship and submission.

I'd heard these two words thrown around a lot, by men, but never it seems in the correct context. Those words are always directed more at the wife/woman when it comes to fulfilling her wifely duties and doing what she was told because the husband is the boss. I'd never heard it preached, taught or seen it lived out loud that both "headship" and "submission" in marriage is about leadership, cooperation and a promise to love, cherish, value, protect and unconditional acceptance God's way. Neither is about ownership, dictatorship or authoritarianism. God's way leads to oneness. It seems the idea of being "large-and-in-charge" gave the husband the right to do whatever, and however he wanted. This same sense of entitlement, I believe, birthed spousal abuse, extramarital affairs, and deception in marriage and beyond.

So, based off the behaviors I'd observed through the years in other marriages and relationships, I made a mental checklist of "If He Ever," and "Things I'm Not Putting Up With." The top non-negotiable is abuse. Along the way I'd learned never to say never because until it's staring you in the face, you don't know what you'd do. That was not the right way to enter a marriage,

I know, but that was where I was and so I struggled. I especially struggled during arguments about sex. This was the only time my husband would quote scripture to me. Yes, all the ones about "wives submit to your own husbands," and my body not being my own. I am fully aware that those directives are in the New Testament and I have no issue with the scriptures. But I took issue with his use of them — during arguments to, I felt, manipulate my behavior. It just solidified my belief that many believe these scriptures to mean that men own their wives.

To have and to hold means you belong to each other not the wife belongs to or is the property of the husband. That is not the society we live in. It is about intimacy — physically and emotionally — with God and each other. It's about staying connected. Sex was designed by God for marriage, so naturally it is an important part of intimacy. It is not end all in a relationship. Ever wonder if sex is taken out of the equation, how many marriages would remain intact? Marriage needs more than physical sex to survive. If you take away the sex, could you stay together?

Intimacy requires two people knowing each other deeply (their heart), being free and open. That's emotional and spiritual, as well as physical. It's the kind of intimacy Adam and Eve had with God in the garden of Eden. God walked and talked with them in the cool of the garden. The Bible doesn't say, but in my imagination, I believe God shared many things with Adam and Eve. The relationship was one of parent and child plus reverence (which is why they hid from his presence after they sinned). Because God created them, he knew them, poured into them, and supported them. (I mean I'll never understand how Adam came up with hippopotamus and platypus) God gave them instructions — not to eat from the tree of the knowledge of good and evil. The relationship was open and honest — naked and unashamed.

So, in case you are still wondering… yes, you can have intimacy without sex. When there is sex without emotional intimacy one, if not both, is left feeling unsafe and disconnected. These feelings often spill over into a couple's sex life or lack of. I once heard Bishop T.D. Jakes say, "intimacy means in to me see." That resonated with me because at one point I felt my husband didn't see me, and that I was only there to meet his need for a "help meet." His focus was on his next career move and what he wanted. Each move benefited our family, but it made our relationship fragile at best. A disconnect developed. Once upon a time, we'd finish each other's sentences or verbalize the same thoughts at the same time. We stopped doing that. That same disconnect started spilling over into other areas of our marriage, too.

To have and to hold also speaks of expectations and hopes for the future — together from this day forward.

While we moved forward through the years, I often felt I was moving along alone or dragging him along with me. We moved through years of marriage with no real blueprint or timeline for our marriage or the future. He wanted children, a house with a yard and careers in the military and as a civil servant. His expectation for me was that I would work in my chosen field, since I already had a job after graduation, and support his endeavors on the home front. Within two years, we welcomed our firstborn and bought a house — all while he was away at Army Officer Candidate School. God was gracious and favored us. Three years later our son was born, and his military career kicked into high gear. I continued to work full-time and rear the children while keeping them involved in community sports and other things they enjoyed. It was my greatest pleasure watching them grow and develop.

From this Day Forward

But I felt unsettled. My behavior ranged from sometimes quarrelsome, belittling and disrespectful, and perhaps worst of all, guarded. A majority of the time, I settled and just did the best I knew how, going along with what he wanted or his directives even when it meant losing myself or being filled with regret. I came to realize that at some point my dreams — other than being a mother — were deferred, and then forgotten because I was never asked about them. I went along with what he wanted because most times it was just easier. In hindsight it was easier for him because he was doing all the things he wanted to do. I didn't resent him being absent more than he was present. Sometimes it was a great blessing. What I was mostly was tired of doing EVERYTHING without him.

Unlike my husband, who has achieved most if not all he planned to do (he had a list before we were married) in his career and "his" life. Next to him I sometimes feel mediocre — neither great nor awful, always pretending to be the "miss independent, "confident extrovert he met in college when inside I was really an insecure ambivert. My grandmother used to tell me that "girls should be seen and not heard." Guess that kind of stuck with me because I've come to understand the look on my face speaks loudly, very loud. Truthfully, I prefer not being seen. Behind the scenes is my favorite place. So, while I've moved along on autopilot supporting my husband and losing pieces of myself. We have accomplished a lot during our thirty years of marriage, but not always together or with the same expectations.

God rebuked me recently while I was whining about being tired of being disappointed and not knowing how much more I could take. We've had many arguments, threatened divorce, and gone to marriage counseling only to find ourselves back at square one months later. It was a blunt reminder that unspoken expectations can't be fulfilled; expectations have to be communicated. After twenty-nine years of ups and downs, feeling lonely and ignored, I finally prayed this prayer: Lord, change my heart and my mind that I might be the wife and helpmeet you are calling me to be. I have messed up time and time again, but you've shown me mercy and grace. Teach me to do the same in my marriage from this day forward.

CHAPTER 3

Leave

If we are going to talk about the principles of marriage, we have to start at the beginning, at Genesis.
"Therefore shall a man leave his father and his mother, and shall cleave unto his wife: and they shall be one flesh." — Genesis 2:24 KJV

The first principle is to "leave" father and mother. Sounds easy enough but leaving is more than just moving out your parents' house and into your own. The intent behind leaving is to set priorities in the new relationship between husband and wife.

The original Hebrew word for leave is *azab*, [aw-zab'], which means to depart from, leave behind or let alone; Merriam-Webster defines leave as "to break apart from." Leaving mother and father doesn't mean disrespecting or dishonoring them. It means they no longer hold the top spot in the life of a new husband or new wife. They — husband and wife — are to put each other first before parents, siblings, other family members and friends. The new order is God, spouse, and then family and friends.

This allows for an adjustment or settling in period for the newlyweds. In fact, this time is so important that Deuteronomy 24:5 says, *"If a man has recently married, he must not be sent to war or have any other duty laid on him. For one year he is to be free to stay at home and bring happiness to the wife he has married."* While that is not be feasible in today's society, the intent is the same — to give the couple a chance to get to know each other and begin to build their marriage without interference.

Adam had no earthly father or mother. Everything Adam needed God provided. Everything Adam needed to know; God taught him. God gave Adam his first job — dressing and caring for the garden. God didn't stop there; he gave Adam dominion (rule) over everything around him. His only relationship was with God, who gave him freedoms and choices. Adam was free to name every living creature what he wanted. Adam was free to eat from every tree in the garden except one. Scripture tells us that every tree, including the tree of life and the tree of knowledge of good and evil, was "pleasant to the sight, and good for food." But Adam was commanded NOT to eat the tree of knowledge of good and evil or there would be dire consequences.

It is safe to say Adam unknowingly learned to be a father from God's example. In his Father's house (the garden), Adam was provided for, nurtured, trained, instructed, and corrected. Adam was even given boundaries. The only thing Adam couldn't do, besides eat from the tree of knowledge of good and evil, was fulfill God's command to be fruitful and multiply. There was no other human there with him. Scriptures do not tell us how long Adam lived in the garden alone or how old he was when God made Woman. Whatever the case, God must have felt his son was ready for a wife so that he too could be fruitful and expand the family.

Scripture also doesn't say how long God took to mold and prepare this woman for Adam after he took a rib from his side. It does say that God brought her to Adam. Sounds a lot like a father walking his daughter down the aisle to meet her groom on their wedding day. This was the first recorded wedding.

Adam happily received his gift from God. Based on his reaction, she brought Adam joy. He proclaimed "this is now . . ." In other words, "now there is someone like me for me." He calls her Woman. The Hebrew word for woman is 'ishah, which means "taken out of." Genesis 2:23 says, "she shall be called Woman, because she was taken out of Man."

No longer alone, Adam now has a wife. He must now prioritize caring for his wife and doing his job taking care of the garden. Paul puts it this way in 1 Corinthians 7:33, *"But he that is married cater for the things that are of the world, how he may please his wife."* Until now Adam only worried pleasing God. Now that he has a wife, the principle of leaving can be put into effect. The two did not leave God's presence, but instead depended on God even more as they learned to love and care for each other. As Father, God most likely did not interfere in their marriage, but gave them space to be physically intimate, but never so far away that they couldn't call out and ask questions.

Likewise, that should now become the role of parents: to be there if needed and offer advice only when asked. Every decision a couple makes, whether it's financial, emotional, spiritual or physical is their decision. Mom and dad's opinion should never outweigh that of a spouse. Again, the spouse is now a top priority. Otherwise some serious stressors and problems may arise, including a breakdown in communication between husband and wife.

Interesting fact: research by Slater and Gordon, a British law firm, found that in-laws were the cause of sixty percent of the arguments in marriages. The top contenders included in-laws giving unsolicited advice and opinions, spouses taking sides with their parents and disagreements over raising children. Sadly, some of this butting-in led many couples to divorce because one chose not to stand up for the other.

Everything about the wedding day and the marriage that proceeds is about choice. A choice of wife (husband) and a choice to accept the responsibilities that come with marriage. I'm reminded of the story of Isaac and Rebekah. Abraham sent his servant to find his son a wife. His servant prayed that the woman God wanted to be Isaac's wife would be kind. And before he concluded his prayer Rebekah shows up. After appealing to her family, Rebekah agrees to go with him. This young woman chooses to travel hundreds of miles by camel to marry a man she'd never seen or met. When she sees Isaac for the first time, she covers her face and waits for the introduction after which Isaac consummates the marriage (Genesis 24). Scriptures say Isaac loved and prayed for Rebekah. It looks like he prayed for 20 years for them to have children. (He was forty when he got married and sixty when Esau and Jacob were born. Genesis 25:19-27). Isaac did not get frustrated or tired of his wife because she hadn't given him sons. Nor did he take another wife or concubine. He made a choice to love and stay with his wife.

The commitment made by way of marriage covenant is to have and to hold from that day forward, for better for worse, for richer for poorer in sickness and in health to love and to cherish till death. From the wedding day forward, the newlyweds choose to love, be gentle with, and giving – not taking, grabbing, or demanding.

A husband must choose to eat his wife's cooking and not compare her skills to his mother's. Just like a wife shouldn't compare her husband to old boyfriends or her father. Comparisons like these are selfish and prideful; comparison robs a spouse of his joy and self-esteem. Spouses must also choose carefully what they share with parents and friends. No one should have a bedside seat to the inner workings of a couple's marriage. It's a recipe for division when the goal is to strengthen a new bond.

Marriage is to be both intimate and exclusive. Webster's defines intimate as "confidant: one to whom secrets are entrusted." Husband and wife are to be each other's confidants. It is okay to have a friend or two of the same sex, but they must respect the boundaries of marriage as should spouses. In other words, what goes on between married couples — intimate details and inner workings — should stay between the couple. Past secrets, however, should not be carried into the marriage. Doing so is an indication of not leaving the past. This is sure to create trust issues between husband and wife before the marriage has any footing. Accepting a marriage proposal means the person being asked is deemed trustworthy, empathetic, patient, caring and supportive — all the qualities of a confidant.

Adam and Eve had to work together in the garden. I believe there were things Adam had to teach his wife and vice versa. Consider this: Adam and Eve were created not birthed; they were created in the image of God. He placed certain innate or natural abilities inside them based on their differences and their similarities. For instance, it is natural for men to be fixers while women are more nurturing. Either way they had to be willing to learn from each other and did so by sharing ideas, information and emotions — communicating.

So, the principle of "leaving" is this:

- A husband and wife must set boundaries, especially for family and friends

- A husband and wife must commit to and become fully dependent on God and each other

- A husband and wife must cultivate their relationship, choosing each other over everyone and everything else

- A husband and wife must not play the comparison game; to do so causes insecurities and tatters trust

- A husband and wife must create blueprints for their marriage

Application:

1. Do create your own traditions while finding ways to celebrate the one's you each grew up with.

2. Don't allow the opinions of others to force you into decisions like having children, etc. The decision is yours alone.

3. Do find a seasoned married couple you both respect and can trust, especially to tell you when you are right or wrong.

First you leave, then you cleave.

CHAPTER 4

Cleave

For Better For Worse

So, what does it mean to "cleave?" Cleave, in Hebrew and according to Merriam-Webster, means "to adhere firmly and closely or loyally and unwaveringly; to cling, to join, to stick."

This principle is one many seem too happy to disregard thanks to a little old thing called "a bill of divorcement." Jesus clarified that "the bill of divorcement" in the New Testament (Mark 10:5) was not his doing. He said Moses added that law because of man's hard heart. In verse seven of that same chapter he repeats, what I believe is his intent for marriage, Genesis 2:24, "Therefore, shall a man leave his father and his mother, and shall cleave unto his wife: and they shall become one flesh." Simply put, cleaving is till death do us part like Adam and Eve.

I think this principle is where the bulk of the wedding vows come into play. Let's look at them.

The Bible doesn't say how long Adam and Eve were married before trouble hit their house. But it is rather interesting that the serpent doesn't show up until AFTER Adam and Eve are married (Genesis 3:1). The serpent gets Eve's attention by introducing doubt and lust. The serpent brings confusion, deception, lies, disobedience, and temptation that immediately strains a marriage that had been intimate and harmonious. The turmoil ultimately separates them from God.

Adam and Eve's marriage had to be one of great intimacy because it was just them and God. With no distractions or previous relationships, the first couple was faithful to each other and God. Since Eve was created to be a "helpmeet," which means "one who is helper and companion," it is reasonable to think that she joined Adam in tending the garden and caring for their home and each other's needs.

"And they were both naked, the man and his wife, and were not ashamed." —Genesis 2:25

Naked is not just the lack of clothing but is also about being bare and unarmed. In other words, they were open with their thoughts and emotions with each other, vulnerable. They weren't worried about appearing weak or being condemned for their feelings or frailties. A far cry from today's societal teachings where young boys are told men don't cry and to keep their guards up while young girls grow up being told it's normal for men to be unfaithful.

The nakedness Adam and Eve had with each other was meant to create an atmosphere of trust, love, and security which is what God delighted in. He still desires this for marriages. But, when satan slithered into the garden (Genesis 3) disobedience didn't only open their eyes to their physical nakedness, but shame and blame entered too.

First, we see the couple try and cover their disobedience and then hide from God when he comes looking to spend time with them. Shame.

"...and they sewed fill leaves together, and made themselves aprons." — Genesis 3:7

Take note, they were together sewing the fig leaves to make aprons just like they were together when Eve picked the fruit from the tree of knowledge of good and evil. They hid together. But once God began to deal with Adam, Adam begins to blame his wife — the same woman he was supposed to nurture, protect and encourage in the Lord. He uncovered or as we say he "threw her under the bus." Adam could have redirected Eve's hand preventing her from not just taking the fruit, but from eating it as well. He was "with her and did eat."

But, instead of admitting that he hadn't stopped her, he left Eve exposed, ashamed, alone and now wounded to deal with the choices they made together. Like her husband, Eve deflected and quickly, and rightfully blamed the serpent.

However, Adam and Eve knew there was a consequence for disobeying God's commands. The serpent convinced the couple that they wouldn't surely die, even though God told them they would. The death wasn't just natural, but a spiritual one as well. A death that would separate them from God. Again, the serpent twisted God's Words to fit his motive — to destroy God's creation: family. He convinced the couple that they wouldn't immediately die. They meant too much to God. Did he lie? Yes and no. Adam lived to be nine-hundred-and-thirty, but his intimate relationship with God died. The marriage is now broken, and its dynamics have changed because Adam blamed Eve for his eating the forbidden fruit instead of taking responsibility for not covering her.

If Adam and Eve lived today, they may be headed to divorce court on the grounds of unreasonable behavior and lack of communication or remain married, but unhappy living separate lives barely speaking to each other. According to United States Divorce Statistics, forty-two percent of first marriages end after about eight years.

So, the question becomes, what does for better or for worse mean? Basically, is being realistic and expecting both good and bad things to happen over the course of a marriage. It will look different for every marriage. Worse may be financial struggles, difficulty in having a child, loss of jobs or shattered dreams. Worse for Adam and Eve was getting kicked out of the garden — the only home they'd ever known — as part of their judgement (punishment) for disobeying God. Worse was also having one son murdered by the other and then being exiled for it. As far as we can tell, Adam and Eve remained together for better, for worse.

For Richer For Poorer

The Bible doesn't give us a picture of what kind of marriage Adam and Eve had after being banned from Eden. But, it was clear they cleaved to each other because even after the murder of Abel, they had more children.

Adam's judgement was that he would have "to sweat" while he worked the fields in order to feed himself, Eve and the children they would have. That certainly was not something he was used to doing. He'd been gardening and eating from plants he hadn't planted. Adam and Eve faced a "for richer, for poorer" scenario because sin entered the earth.

For certain Eve had to come to a place of trust. Adam would be responsible for providing for her, protecting and caring for her in spite of their circumstances in this new environment.

Perhaps she even accepted that Adam's rule over her was not meant to be about control but headship (leadership) since he was the one that God originally gave His commands.

So how does Adam step up as a leader?

First, Adam affirms her. In Genesis 3:20, Adam names his wife Eve. Until now she was only referred to as "Woman." Giving her a name represented the same authority he used when naming the animals in the garden. Affirming her also showed his commitment as her husband to love and care for her despite their circumstances. It also showed his belief in the promise God made that they would bring forth children: Eve means mother of all living.

Couples today, especially women, have great expectations of being cared for and building for the future. But, all too often those expectations aren't shared or discussed with their husbands before marriage. Then after the wedding the couple struggles with not having or doing the things they see others doing. I mean who hasn't seen couples walking along the sidewalk or in the park holding hands and looking at each other like they were the best thing since sliced bread and not felt a twinge of envy because that's not what you get to enjoy. In the early years of my marriage, I longed to hold hands and sneak kisses in public with my husband, but he would rebuff me because he "didn't do public displays of affection." What he didn't realize was that he didn't do it behind closed doors either. Unrequited love, perceived, or not, even in a marriage can cause pain, grief and shame which often leads to stress and arguments.

Adam has now become a "poor man" because of sin. He's forced to leave the beautiful home and life he'd been given and go out and build one. He took responsibility for his actions in not stopping Eve from taking the fruit from the tree and eating it, instead of continuing to blame her.

In Sickness and In Health

The second thing Adam did to step up as the leader in his family was to stay with her. Even though Eve was tricked by the serpent, she was still his gift from God, his wife. He also heard God tell Eve that she would have sorrow [pain, labor] giving birth. That didn't sway Adam's decision to stay. Perhaps having watched the animals in the garden give birth, he understood that there was a chance Eve could become sick or die while giving birth.

Sadly, researchers have found that 75 percent of couples that deal with chronic illnesses end in divorce. A study from Iowa State University found that "women diagnosed with serious illnesses like cancer are at a higher risk of divorce, but not so when it is the man that becomes sick."

In my years of living I've had several bouts with illness and came out victorious. I'll never forget my last major surgery. The surgeon teased me about his consult with my husband after the removal of a goiter on my thyroid. According to my doctors it could have suffocated me in sleep because it was enlarging around my windpipe. The doctor said when he told my husband that they removed my thyroid and I was in recovery doing well that he started to cry and ask how and what care I would need. My mother offered to come and help for me. He told her that she was welcome to come and sit with me, but that caring for me was his responsibility. My mother, not one to argue, agreed but was there to help when he was at work. Other than the birth of our first born (he had to return to active duty the day after she was born), he has been present to care and nurse me back to health.

Remaining in a marriage during sickness can be hard, but love and commitment should always win. This is why marriage should not be entered into lightly. It is a covenant relationship between God, husband and wife. It was only meant to be broken by death.

Scriptures don't say that Eve got sick in childbirth nor does it mention losing any children in the childbirth process. We learn that Adam and Eve were the parents of Cain, Abel and Seth; they had other children that are not named. We learn about Abel's murder by his brother, but we don't get a view of Adam and Eve's relationship after this. One can only guess that they weathered another unfamiliar storm with love and care. Adam was 130 years old when Seth was born.

Scriptures never give us Eve's age; we only know that Adam had more children after Seth and that he was 930 years old when he died.

If Adam and Eve aren't enough to convince you about leaving and cleaving, look to Jacob. Jacob fell in love with Rachel before she reached him at the well after he tricked his brother out of his blessing. He discovered the young woman was from his mother's family and he went in pursuit of her. What was supposed to be seven years turned into fourteen and two wives instead of one.

Only problem is he loved one and despised the other. Even in his anger with Rachel for demanding he give her children; he still loved and did his best to make her happy — even going as far as sleeping with her maid when she spent years barren. (Read this story in Genesis 29-35). I'm not advocating that kind of behavior. I'm simply pointing out what Jacob may have perceived as sacrificial love. He was with her until her death.

So, the principle of "cleaving" is this:

- A husband and wife remain committed during lack and plenty

- A husband and wife must care for each other in sickness and good health

- A husband and wife must nourish intimacy — physical, spiritual, and emotional

- A husband and wife are their children's teachers, especially from the spiritual point of view

- A husband and wife must forge a full partnership

Application:

1. Remember marriage is a covenant not a contract. Practice forgiveness and extend grace often.

2. Couples have arguments. Do not run to your parents or friends with an overnight bag because you had a disagreement. Take some time and then sit down and talk to each other.

3. Be sure to invest and support each other's dreams and passions.

4. Don't forget to continue to pursue each other.

Leave, then cleave and become one.

MY HEADLESS MARRIAGE

CHAPTER 5

Becoming One

There is a profound scene in Tyler Perry's Madea's Family Reunion where Aunt Myrtle (Cicely Tyson) and May (Maya Angelou) are snapping green beans at the kitchen table discussing marriage with their nieces. Aunt Myrtle is speaking about her marriage to her deceased husband.

"we had a love so strong ... that it just seemed like we were one. I would get ready to tell him something, and he would open his mouth and say the very thing, that I was fixing to tell him. And then there were moments when I would lay my head on his chest just to listen to his heartbeat. And then one night, I realized that his heart beat matched mine."— Aunt Myrtle

Becoming one is the last of God's principles for marriage: two individuals "shall be one flesh." — Genesis 2:24. I've heard it said that this happens after you say I do. That is not true. Becoming one is not an instantaneous act, but rather a process. Why a process? Because marriage involves two individuals choosing to form a single unit. No more me or my, but we, us and ours.

The word shall is future tense and expresses an intention, command. Just as shall is futuristic, flesh is more than physical gratification. Flesh, in this context, denotes unity not just a physical (covenant) joining of two bodies in the act of intercourse. But it is a merging of two lives, two mindsets if you will, that will result in children who one day will do the same and replenish the earth. So, to think that "two shall be one" is automatic is unrealistic. As unrealistic as fairy tales. To get to oneness takes more effort than combining household furniture and bank accounts.

The journey to becoming unified involves sacrifice, compromise, communication, and demonstration. It also requires leadership and submission. Most importantly it requires prayer and spending time together in the Word and getting to know each other better. Becoming one is the couple being so connected that they walk, talk and think alike. They build together, and even, some would say, begin to look favor each other.

Funny story: About 10 years ago, doctors discovered a goiter on my thyroid. It was growing inward and large. So, the decision was made for me to have a thyroidectomy. Later that same year, during a routine checkup, nodules would be discovered on my husband's thyroid. He had to have half of his removed. We take the same medication, but because of our weight and need we take different doses. Talk about a weird example of becoming one.

Anyway . . . this is why exclusivity — undivided and restricted — is a necessity. Outside interference will do what God commanded in Matthew 24:51, "put asunder." Asunder: to place room between, separate. No one or nothing should be able to come between you. The serpent didn't separate Adam and Eve. In fact, they were together when he started pouring doubt into Eve's mind. He used lust and pride to distract and confuse her. Ever noticed that scripture never mentions the serpent or satan bothering Adam while he was alone in the garden?

Satan didn't rear his head until the man and woman became a couple, a family. He devised a plan to destroy the family God was creating for himself. I believe he didn't really care about separating them from each other; satan's goal was to separate them from God. He succeeded in doing that. Temporarily. They remained committed to God's instructions for their lives and their marriage.

They'd experienced their first conflict. But with God showing mercy and unconditional love for them, we can only guess that they did the same for each other. In marriage there will be conflict, and there will be times you won't agree. This is where prayer, compromise and communication will be important tools for resolution.

It would be many years later that the idea of divorce surfaces in scriptures. And Jesus was clear that divorce was a man-idea and not a God-idea. Deuteronomy 24:1 says "that if a woman loses favor with her husband and he's found some uncleanness in her he can write her a bill of divorcement." A few things to note divorce wasn't about adultery. Adultery was punishable by stoning. The word "uncleanness" has nothing to do with being physically dirty but refers to disgrace or shame. That could be something as simple as embarrassment like Queen Vashti did to King Xerxes in the book of Esther when she wouldn't be paraded in front of his cohorts. Or maybe in modern times burning dinner and having an unkept house. But it's clear that divorce like not "leaving" is considered an option when things get tough in marriage.

Let's be clear: Marriage is not a mathematical equation of 1/2+1/2=1. That's why it is important for men and women to be whole and ready for marriage. It is not as the old cliché goes — that your spouse is your better half. No ma'am and sirs. The goal is for you to make each other better people and you can only do that if you are whole. Don't get me wrong. I am not talking about not having "issues." I am talking about baggage and weights that are keeping you from being your best self. For instance, if you have trust issues how are you going to trust your husband/wife? Deal with that before you say, "I do." Marriage takes lots of work to get to "and they shall be one flesh." I have to believe also that Adam and Even continued their journey growing together, respecting and honoring each other's differences.

Imagine the wisdom and life lessons Adam and Eve must have gained during their years of marriage. Even though they disobeyed God's command not to eat from the tree of knowledge of good and evil, they fulfilled his principles of marriage: leave, cleave and become one.

God's intention was for marriage to last a lifetime between one man and one woman, the two becoming inseparable.

Here's the final look at the traditional wedding vows. The words that come after "in sickness and in health." Those words are: "to love, cherish, and obey, till death us do part, according to God's holy law."

Interesting fact: On Septembers 12, 1922, the Episcopal Church voted to remove the word "obey" from the bride's portion of the wedding vows. No real explanation found. But I thought that was very interesting, especially since you rarely hear "obey" during the wedding vows anymore.

Obey is defined as "to comply with the command, direction or request." A word we freely use with our children, but don't want to hear from a spouse. But obey simply means to submit, to choose to not overtly resist to your husband's will. Took a lot of tears for me to understand that submission doesn't make me weak or less than but it shows strength of character.

So, the principle of "two becoming one" is this:

·• A husband and wife must work as a team; there is no more me or I, but it's we, us and our

• A husband and wife must honor and respect each other

• A husband and wife must resolve their problems and make decisions together

• A husband and wife must respect their differences and learn from each other

Application:

1. Do have regular family meetings and assess your marriage. Wives should be a reflection of her husband; husbands should be a reflection of Christ.

2. Don't be afraid of getting a marriage tune-up from a reputable counselor or therapist.

3. Be intentional about honoring and respecting each other even when he/she does something you don't agree with or hurts your feelings.

CHAPTER 6

Headship

The road to oneness was probably much easier for Adam and Eve than it is for most of us today considering all the scriptural instructions for wives and husbands beginning with Adam and Eve's judgement. Whether Eve struggled with God's sentence in Genesis 3:16, it's not known. Her sentence was this: "that her desire would be for Adam and that Adam would rule over her." There are two thoughts about desire — sexual desire and desire for control.

The Hebrew meaning of desire is longing and stretching out after. Perhaps the interpretation behind the desire for control is linked to Eve's passing the forbidden fruit to Adam to eat (seen as an act of leading). We see the use of the word desire again in Genesis 4:7 when God tells Cain that if he does well, what is pleasing then he would be accepted, but if not sin would overtake him, if he didn't master his feelings. Needless to say, Cain didn't control his emotions.

Maybe Eve's sentence wasn't as bad as it sounded. In fact, it was God's way of setting things back in order. He created Adam, gave him rules, instructions, and authority. Adam relinquished his responsibilities by doing the very thing God told him not to do. Adam having rule over Eve was a glimpse into what leadership and submission was supposed to be.

Adam represented headship. Headship is a position of responsibility and authority. As stated earlier, Adam was given the responsibility to care for the garden, name the animals and eventually name Eve, his suitable helper. It was Adam God held responsible for he and Eve sinning. After expulsion from the garden, Adam is tasked to work the ground and provide for his wife and eventually children.

Somewhere along the way, the world once again got out of order when it comes to God's plan for marriage. Christians quote scriptures about marriage, but rarely teach by example what it should look like according to God's way. Earlier I stated that it was something I've struggled with. The struggle isn't with the command, but the mishandling of the position. All my life I've heard the term headship and submission used in such negative ways that it made me never want to be married and have a bit of disdain for the word itself because of a lack of understanding. Headship is not about controlling or wielding the "do as I say because I am your husband/the head."

It is not about a division of household chores — the woman cooks and cleans and the man takes out the trash or cuts the grass, etc. These attitudes of dictatorship have damaged many marriage relationships because the husband, while it may not have been his intent, demeaned and devalued his wife. Such behavior forces a wife into submission and sows bitterness and resentment and breeds disrespect. This is especially true if he is one that uses scriptures to coerce each other into submission. Society has taken those two words and mishandled them. Men use both to exert power and authority over women. That power trip often leads to both physical and verbal abuse and has long lasting effects. Let's take Abraham and Sarah's story.

Abraham was promised that he would be the father of many nations, but he and Sarah had no children. Because of their ages and the long wait for the promise to manifest, Sarah convinced Abraham to sleep with her maid in hopes of her getting pregnant with a son.

It's the whole forbidden fruit all over again. Instead of saying no to Sarah and encouraging her to wait on the Lord, Abraham gave in to the flesh. Then he puts the responsibility of the pregnant girl back on Sarah when she starts to complain about Hagar's attitude; Hagar becoming pregnant becomes a point of contention between the two women; feelings of jealousy and bitterness growing in both. Ishmael was not the promised child, but he was included in God's grace toward the nations that would come from both sons. Ishmael is the father of twelve tribes just like Isaac. And today the descendants — Jews and Muslims — of these two men continue to fight with each other over who is the rightful heir of promise.

My husband said to me on one occasion that I was to do whatever he said as long as it wasn't immoral or illegal and he would have to be held accountable for it. The story of Ananias and Sapphira in Acts 5 convinced me that wasn't completely true. The Scriptures tell us that Ananias sold property and with his wife's knowledge kept some of the proceeds from the sale instead of giving it all to Peter. As the story goes, he shows up first at the meeting place. Peter discerns what Ananias has done and Ananias drops dead and his body is carried out. Three hours later Sapphira shows up and maintains her husband's lie when she could have simply told the truth. Peter tells her what has happened to her husband and then she falls dead, too. This tells me that as a wife I need to pray and trust God for the right answer and not just be complicit, especially with a lie. At the same time, I can't be so stubborn and headstrong that I can't hear his heart.

Knowing this, I've disagreed on many occasions. My perceived disobedience has led to many arguments and even threats of divorce. It has taken 30 years of marriage for me to fully understand that my problem is not an issue with authority or that I don't know how to submit, but rather that I've been in a "headless" marriage.

Headship is both a position of authority and a call. A call to love unselfishly and unconditionally. Paul says in Ephesians 5:25-30 that husbands are to love their wives like Christ loved the church and as they love their own bodies. Christ died for the church unselfishly. He didn't put any pressure on the church because He did; He died willingly because of love.

From the beginning, man was given free will to choose right from wrong. He said to be holy [dedicated to God, set apart]. He certainly didn't physically or emotionally abuse the church because he loves her.

No, in fact, not only did he die for her, but he sent Holy Spirit to comfort, lead and guide her. Headship requires men (and women) to be imitators of God.

My husband is a great provider and good father, but from the very beginning relinquished many of his leadership responsibilities. He has described his leadership style as "hands-off." That basically means 'you handle it until you do something I don't like, then I'll say something or take over.' It also boiled down to me running a household, raising children, working full-time, planning everything, and being a 24-7 ego booster. For years I thought being "superwoman" didn't bother me, but the more he was absent the more I began to lose myself, feel empty and unfulfilled. Yet, I was expected to continue to pour in to him.

When I failed to do what he wants or suggest something else, I am accused of wanting to be the head, in control or to make "it" about me. Sometimes I do want it to be about me, I won't lie. Because for most of our marriage it hasn't been. I've always known that my happiness was not his responsibility, but it can be pretty easy to look at your spouse and place blame rather than accepting responsibility for what you are not doing. This is what my good, good Father chastised me about. Instead of complaining about what he wasn't doing, I started praying to help me be a better person, wife and mother. If I wanted change it had to start within me in order to get what I desired most.

What I want, is Christlike leadership. Leadership that is as concerned about my spiritual and physical well-being. Leadership that studied the Word in private and with the family. This has been a point of contention. Ephesians 5:25-27, says husband's must know the Word in order to relate to his wife. Why?

"Husbands, love your wives, just as Christ loved the church and gave himself up for her to make her holy, cleansing her by the washing with water through the word, and to present her to himself as a radiant church, without stain or wrinkle or any other blemish, but holy and blameless."

To wash is not about cleaning up, it is about making sure she grows spiritually, that she conquers her insecurities and feels supported. For the first year of marriage, we rarely attended church and he was okay with that. I wasn't. I grew up being actively involved in church from singing in the choir to assisting in Sunday School. He never stopped me from going, but he never made a point of saying, "let's find a church home." The more I grew in the Word, the more he felt I was choosing "church" over him. I won't go into detail, but I will say some of the things said during arguments left me feeling unloved and trust broken. That was not the leadership I desired or that God requires of us. It was like I pictured Eve when Adam told God, "This woman you gave me" caused him to sin. Adam's words, though true, left Eve unprotected and probably feeling insecure about herself and their relationship.

Leadership also did not look like offense every time I shared my feelings. Leadership looks like listening with open ears and mind seeking to understand not play the blame game when the conversation gets uncomfortable. Because I can be emotional and sometimes very blunt, the Lord has to chastise me. On one of these occasions, He taught me how to apologize. Apologizing is all about taking ownership of your behavior and words. I was instructed to never again say I'm sorry, but instead to ask for forgiveness for specifically what I'd done. Not all that "if I (did this or that)."

Leadership sees a need and fills it rather than having to be always be asked. It is about being present physically and emotionally not to just have your needs met, but to be aware of what affects the wife and family. 1 Peter 3:7 instructs husbands "dwell with them according to knowledge, giving honor unto the wife." Knowledge requires talking to her, getting to know her — outside the bedroom. I saw a quote I liked from the late rapper, activist and entrepreneur Nipsey Hussle: "study your queen so you can give her what she wants without her asking." That applies to more than just stuff.

Knowledge requires being present not just there. Being present is more than just being in the house. Present is to be in the moment, listening, hearing and being actively involved. One of the reasons pastor kids have a reputation of being wild, and rebellious is because the fathers (sometimes mothers) are typically out ministering to everybody but those he/she lives with; the call to preach and/or pastor to others seems more important than minister to their first call — their families. Not sure what Aaron and Eli had going on; they had sons offering strange fire and having sex with congregants in the tabernacle/temple. They all died. I digress. Not being present causes you to miss not just what someone is sharing verbally; it's also paying attention to what they aren't. Body language and expressions can often speak louder than words, especially when it comes to children. When leadership mimics Christ, submission, respect and honor come easy. However, when it doesn't guess what? Wives must still do these things. A life of submission is transformative. 1 Corinthians 7:16 says, "how do you know whether you will save your husband." As wives, our beauty is not to be outward only. Like Rebekah we should be kind, not pushy or a nag, and be cautious with her words. Nobody wants to be called a contentious woman.

I'm trying to get better in all areas. I've had to step back and accept responsibility for the role I played in living in a headless marriage. My role was to be both helpmeet and neck. The role of the neck is to support the head. It houses the blood supply to the brain from the heart. As strong as the neck is, it is fragile.

Adam was charged with being Eve's covering, protector, provider, friend and lover. And was to be the lead teacher for his family. We get a glimpse of that outside the safety of the garden, Adam taught his children about God. How so? Cain and Abel knew to offer sacrifices to God. Who other than Adam could have taught them that?

The story of man's fall is often stopped at God putting them out of the garden. It isn't shown that though he fell, Adam got back up and accepted responsibility for his wife and received back the authority given to him.

What was a pitiful show of the blame game turned out to be the first story of love and redemption. Eve went from being in a headless marriage to a marriage that lasted a lifetime based on God's principles for marriage — to leave, cleave and become one.

A married couple's journey to oneness should be reflection of Jesus in both their lives. Paul gives us a long list of emotions we should pull off in our journey to being holy. Can I submit that those same things need to come off in marriage: anger rage, malice, slander and foul language. I've exhibited a lot of those emotions over the years to my own detriment. None of that in no wise is respectful or reflects Jesus.

My desire is for all of us to find freedom in what God expects from us as husbands and wives. We are overcomers by the blood of the Lamb and by the word of our testimony. My testimony after 31 years of marriage is that we are a work in progress. In spite of how things began, I am confident that they are evolving because of our willingness to put in the work. The final result will be that we be found without "no spot or wrinkle.

A Final Word

This was one of the hardest things I've written in my life. For one it required a lot of transparency and openness. Also hard was allowing my husband to read this before going to print. I felt he would feel vilified (and he did). That was not my intent.

At the printing of this book, we will have celebrated 31 years of marriage. I have been married longer than I have been an adult. I'd been 21 for seven whole months when I got married. It hasn't always been blissful, but our marriage is blessed because we learned to practice forgiveness. He said he's learned to let me be me. That folks is not always the correct answer. (Laugh out loud). What you have just finished is a testament of my journey in marriage and what I wish I had known. If I can help just one person then my goal will have been achieved.

Please know I am not married to an ogre. My husband has been on a journey, just like I have, to be the best husband he can be to me. My husband has his faults, as do I, but he has been supportive, caring and encouraging over the years. And even when I struggled against him, we toiled together. Learning together, failing together. With God's help we've been victorous in many areas and I can say we are working on the areas where we are and have been the weakest.

Those weak spots are due to not fully leaving the familiar baggage of our past as we strive to be different, do different in the future. But God is a God of restoration and headship in my marriage is being restored. And I am filling the call of the aged woman teaching the younger to love their own husbands and children and to make a home for your family.

DISCUSSION QUESTIONS

1. What are the three principles of marriage, according to Genesis 2:24?

2. Which was harder to do — leave, cleave or become one?

3. Are boundaries necessary for family, and friends? Why?

4. What is intimacy? Is there a difference between intimacy and being present?

5. Do you think wedding vows line up with scripture?

6. Which Bible romance stories exemplify the principles of marriage?

7. Why do you think sickness pulls people apart rather cause them to cleave more?

8. Is becoming one literal or spiritual?

9. Discuss the world's view of headship in comparison to the Bible.

10. What can be a long-term effect of poor headship?

Scripture Index

Genesis
2:24-25
3:7,20
4:7
29-30;
35:16-20
Leviticus
20:10
Deuteronomy
22:22
24:1, 5
2 Samuel
6
Esther
1:10-22
Proverbs
5
Hosea
2:2

Matthew
6:24
19
24:51
Mark
10:11, 12
Luke
16:18
1 Corinthians
7:16, 33
2 Corinthians
13
Ephesians
5:23-30
Titus
2:3-5
Hebrews
12:6
1 Peter
3:7

About the Author

Zelda Oliver-Miles is wife to Wendell and mom to Xenia and Yori. She's authored many articles over the years as a journalist and ghostwriter. This is her second book. Her first was *Amelia Gayle Gorgas: First Woman of Position*; the book is a part of the Alabama Roots Biography Series. Her greatest passion is for all who will come to have a relationship with Jesus Christ. She grew up in the Black Belt towns of Marion and Selma, Alabama and has been writing since she was sixteen. She is a graduate of The University of Alabama.

MY HEADLESS MARRIAGE

www.ingramcontent.com/pod-product-compliance
Lightning Source LLC
Chambersburg PA
CBHW070208100426
42743CB00013B/3099